Stonehenge

and Neighbouring Monuments

R J C Atkinson CBE, MA, FSA
Professor Emeritus of Archaeology,
University College Cardiff

Stonehenge is the most important prehistoric monument in the whole of Britain. It is unique, and there is nothing else like it anywhere in the world. From the earliest times it has aroused the awe of visitors as one of the wonders of Britain.

The monument we see today is the much-ruined final phase of Stonehenge, the prehistoric temple in use some 3500 years ago.

There were three phases in Stonehenge's development.

The first Stonehenge was a large earthwork 'henge' used as a place of Neolithic worship and burial about 5000 years ago.

Almost a thousand years later, in about 2000 BC, Stonehenge was rebuilt using stones from the Preseli Mountains in Wales ('bluestones').

Soon after, the present 'temple' was constructed of much larger stones from the Marlborough Downs (Sarsens) and the bluestones were rearranged within the circle.

It is important to remember that the original entrance to Stonehenge was from the Avenue, a processional way which aligned with the midsummer sunrise in the north-east. The line of the Avenue is marked by the Heel Stone.

This guidebook opens with a fully illustrated description of what the visitor can see today. The remarkable features of Stonehenge are pointed out, and each is cross-referenced to a more detailed account of the monument's construction in the second chapter. The story of the prehistoric peoples who built Stonehenge is told in the third chapter. Finally, the visitor is encouraged to explore the self-guided trails around Stonehenge and see the barrows and other prehistoric sites.

Contents

Left The sarsen circle with its run of continuous lintels, seen from the north-east

8-2-99 G

ENGLISH HERITAGE

Published by ENGLISH HERITAGE

Edited by Ken Osborne, designed by Martin Atcherley and Associates, and typeset by TypeArt in ITC Century Light.

ISBN 1 85074 172 7

Copyright © English Heritage, London, 1987.
This edition first published 1987.
Third impression 1990.

Printed in England by Westerham Press. C1250. 3/90.

Tour of Stonehenge

Stonehenge is a prehistoric temple of unequalled importance. From the earliest times it has aroused the awe and the curiosity of its visitors. It was first mentioned as one of the wonders of Britain only seventy years after the Norman Conquest, and since then almost every people of antiquity has been claimed as its builders, at one time or another.

It is only during the twentieth century that archaeological excavations have yielded reliable information about its history and its age, so that we can now say what the main features of Stonehenge are, and roughly when and in what order they were built.

Today's visitor approaches Stonehenge on its west side. The original ceremonial entrance was from the north-east, leading from the Avenue – a processional way (see plan on page 11). Both the original entrance and the Avenue align with the direction of the midsummer sunrise, but the course of the Avenue is best seen in aerial photographs.

The final stage of Stonehenge which visitors see today is considerably ruined. When complete, Stonehenge consisted of a fully lintelled stone circle, which enclosed an inner horseshoe arrangement of stones, open, perhaps significantly, on the north-east side. Around the stone circle were an earth bank and ditch. The original entrance, no longer visible, is marked by the fallen Slaughter Stone (an original portal stone) and beyond it the famous Heel Stone (above which the midsummer sun passes when viewed from the centre of the stone circle).

What to look for

The standing stones in the centre consist of two main kinds of rock. The larger blocks and their lintels are all of **sarsen**, a natural sandstone which occurs as huge boulders on the surface of the Marlborough Downs about 30km (20 miles) to the north of Stonehenge. The smaller stones, known as the **Bluestones** from their colour, are of several kinds of rock which come from the Preseli Mountains in south-west Wales.

The **Sarsen Circle**, about 30m (100ft) in diameter, consisted originally of 30 uprights, each weighing about 25 tonnes, capped by a continuous ring of 30 lintels weighing about 7 tonnes. Inside it was a horseshoe of five **Sarsen Trilithons** each consisting of a pair of huge uprights, weighing up to 45 tonnes, capped by a massive lintel.

Apart from the Heel Stone, all the sarsens have been dressed to shape by pounding their

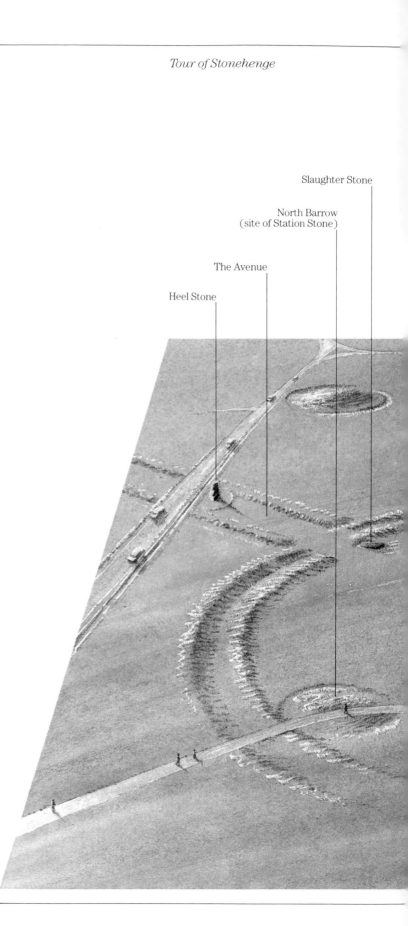

Tour of Stonehenge

Slaughter Stone

North Barrow
(site of Station Stone)

The Avenue

Heel Stone

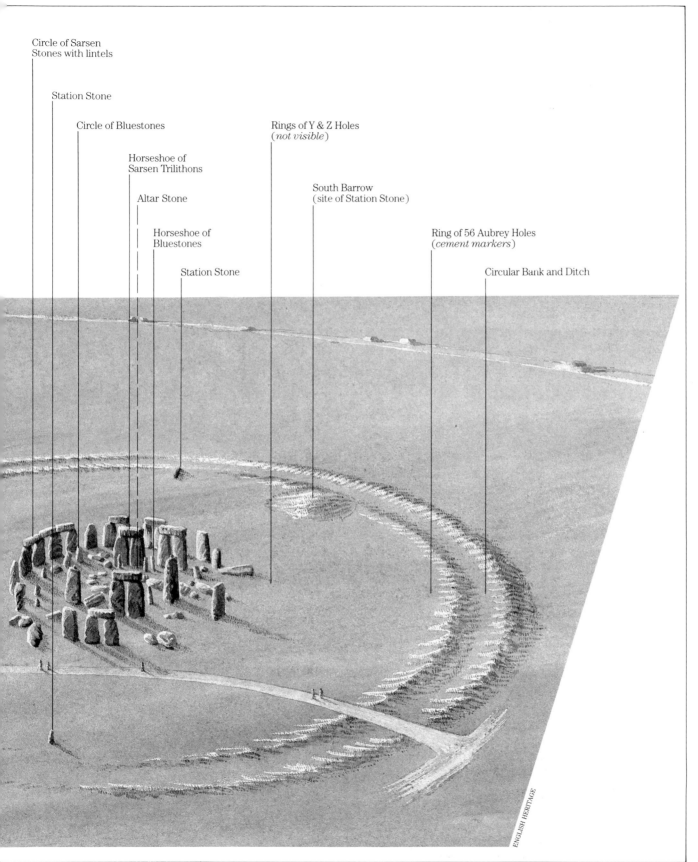

Circle of Sarsen
Stones with lintels

Station Stone

Circle of Bluestones

Horseshoe of
Sarsen Trilithons

Altar Stone

Horseshoe of
Bluestones

Station Stone

Rings of Y & Z Holes
(*not visible*)

South Barrow
(site of Station Stone)

Ring of 56 Aubrey Holes
(*cement markers*)

Circular Bank and Ditch

ENGLISH HERITAGE

Above *Grooved bluestone, forming part of the bluestone horseshoe*

Below *Sarsen circle with, in foreground, five bluestones of the bluestone circle*

surfaces with stone hammers. The uprights are slightly 'dished' on the top to provide a secure seating for the lintels, and tenons have been left projecting from them to fit into corresponding hollow mortice-holes in the undersides of the lintels. In addition, the lintels of the outer circle are fitted to each other with vertical tongue-and-groove joints. (See 'Arrival of the Sarsens' on page 10 and 'How Stonehenge was built' which describes the transport and erection of the sarsen stones on page 15).

The **Bluestone Circle**, now much ruined and incomplete, stands inside the sarsen circle. Originally it consisted of about 60 stones set close together. Only two of the surviving stones have been dressed to shape, and both of these had formerly been used as lintels.

The **Bluestone Horseshoe**, standing inside the sarsen horseshoe, originally had 19 stones which increased in height towards the centre. They have all been dressed to one of two shapes, a square pillar or a tapering obelisk, which alternate round the horseshoe. Two of them bear traces on their tops of projecting tenons, which have been almost battered away. Another

has a dished top, like the sarsen uprights, and the adjacent pillar has a groove worked all the way down one side. This stone must once have fitted against another with a corresponding ridge, which now survives only as a stump below the surface on the opposite side of the horseshoe. (See 'Arrival of Bluestones' on page 9 and 'How Stonehenge was built' which describes the transport of the bluestones on page 15).

At the focus of the bluestone horseshoe is the **Altar Stone**, a dressed block of blue-grey sandstone from the shores of Milford Haven in Pembrokeshire, about 5m (16ft) long. It is now buried in the ground beneath the fallen upright and lintel of the great sarsen trilithon, but originally it probably stood upright as a pillar. Two circles of excavated holes, not visible on the

Opposite *Two trilithons in the sarsen horseshoe, with a bluestone in front. Note the high finish of the uprights, the gentle curving of the lintels and outward inclination of their sides – refinements peculiar to Stonehenge*

Left *The Heel Stone marks the original approach to Stonehenge. It shows the direction of the midsummer sunrise when viewed from the centre*

MICHAEL BLAKE

surface, are shown on the plan just outside the sarsen circle. These are known as the **Y and Z Holes** and they are thought to represent a setting of the bluestones prior to the final arrangement (see page 13).

The visitor should now proceed along the path and turn left to the far side of the circle.

The Earthwork and the Avenue

The outer boundary of Stonehenge is the low circular **bank** which lies about 30m (100ft) outside the stones. Originally it stood about 1.8m (6ft) high and was built of chalk rubble quarried from the **ditch** immediately outside it. In the course of nearly fifty centuries most of it has been weathered down and has slipped back, obscuring the very irregular outlines of the ditch, which originally consisted of a string of rough quarry-pits with steep sides and flat bottoms. One half of the circuit of the ditch was excavated in 1919-26, and was only partly refilled afterwards. The other half remains untouched. (See 'The First Stonehenge' on page 8).

The earthwork is broken by a broad **entrance** on the north-east side, nearest the road, and by some smaller gaps, elsewhere, some of which are modern. From the entrance the **Avenue**, marked by a low bank and ditch on either side, runs downhill across the road and

leads eventually to the bank of the River Avon at West Amesbury. (A fuller description of the Avenue appears on page 9). Within the Avenue, close to the road, stands the **Heel Stone** with traces of a circular ditch around its base. Evidence from an excavation in 1979 suggests that the Heel Stone was paired originally with a second stone.

Just inside the bank is a ring of 56 pits, now filled up, known as the **Aubrey Holes** after their discoverer John Aubrey (1626-97). About half of them have been excavated and are marked by discs of white cement let into the turf.

At the entrance of the earthwork is a large fallen stone, known as the **Slaughter Stone**. It originally stood upright on its outer end and together with a similar stone, now vanished, formed a ceremonial doorway to the site. Further round the earthwork, on the line of the Aubrey Holes, there are two smaller stones, one fallen and one still upright, called the **Station Stones**. Two other stones, now missing, formerly stood at a similar distance inside the bank, each of them in a small ditched enclosure. These are known as the North and South Barrows, though there was no central mound. (For the Aubrey Holes and Slaughter Stone see 'The First Stonehenge' on page 8).

The visitor should retrace his steps by the same route.

Left *In this unique aerial photograph of Stonehenge under snow cover, the true outline of the monument can be clearly seen. Enclosing the stone circle are the bank and ditch. Beyond the stone circle are the Heel Stone and line of the Avenue, cut by the modern road*

ENGLISH HERITAGE

History and Construction of Stonehenge

As in many later cathedrals and churches, not all the structures that we see today at Stonehenge were built at the same time. As the result of excavations we can now divide the history of Stonehenge into several periods, covering a span of about twenty centuries between about 3100 and 1100 BC.

The First Stonehenge

3000 BC   2000 BC   1000 BC

The earliest structures were the bank, ditch and the Aubrey Holes, all probably built about 3100 BC. There was probably some kind of gateway or ceremonial arch of timber a little to the west of the present Heel Stone, on the axis of the circular earthwork, and a pair of small stones standing in the middle of the entrance, forming a doorway without a lintel. Perhaps too there was some small building of timber, or a setting of stones, at the centre, an area long since destroyed by treasure-hunters.

The Aubrey Holes are round pits in the chalk about one metre wide and deep, with steep sides and flat bottoms, forming a circle about 86.6m (284ft) in diameter. They seem to have been filled up very soon after they were dug. Later, cremated human bones were buried in smaller holes made in the chalk filling; but there is no reason to suppose that they were made as graves in the first place, or that they ever held uprights of wood or stone. They probably represent some kind of magical or religious ceremony, of which we shall never know the details.

It is possible that the four Station Stones belong to this period also, but the evidence is uncertain.

Below The first Stonehenge comprised the bank and ditch enclosing the Aubrey Holes. There was probably a ceremonial gateway on roughly the present alignment. There may have been a timber building in the centre, but no evidence for this survives. The site was built around 3100BC, but was in use for only about 500 years, after which it reverted to scrub

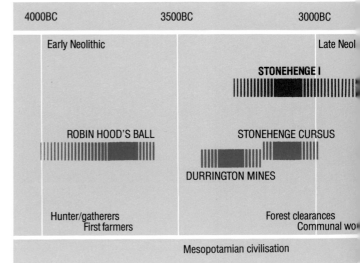

ENGLISH HERITAGE

Right Time chart showing the stages of Stonehenge with neighbouring monuments of the prehistoric period

4000BC	3500BC	3000BC
Early Neolithic		Late Neol
		STONEHENGE I
ROBIN HOOD'S BALL	STONEHENGE CURSUS	
	DURRINGTON MINES	
Hunter/gatherers	Forest clearances	
First farmers	Communal wo	
Mesopotamian civilisation		

A few similar open-air temples of much smaller size, containing rings of pits with cremated burials, have been found elsewhere in Britain. Like the first Stonehenge, they all probably belong to the Late Neolithic period.

Arrival of the Bluestones

3000 BC   2000 BC   1000 BC

Some time after Period I, Stonehenge was abandoned and the site reverted to scrub, but around 2100 BC Stonehenge was radically remodelled. About 80 bluestones, weighing up to 4 tonnes apiece, were to be set up to form two circles, one inside the other, round the centre of the site. There was an entrance, pointing towards the rising sun at mid-summer, marked externally by a pair of Heel Stones and by extra stones on the inside; and on the opposite side a large pit may have held a bluestone of exceptional size, perhaps the present Altar Stone. There was also some kind of interior setting, possibly a horseshoe, of which only a few holes are known. The bluestones may have been brought to Stonehenge from some undiscovered site in Wiltshire to which they had been transported centuries before for another purpose. Excavations have shown, however, that this double circle was never finished and that for at least a quarter of its circumference on the west side the stones were not set up.

At the same time the original entrance of the

Below *The second development stage occurred around 2100BC when Stonehenge was radically remodelled. Some 80 bluestones from the Preseli mountains in south-west Wales were set up at the centre, forming an incomplete double circle. The entrance was widened and a pair of Heel Stones erected. The nearer part of the Avenue was built, aligned with the midsummer sunrise*

ENGLISH HERITAGE

circular earthwork was widened by throwing about 8m (25ft) of the bank back into the ditch on the east side. From here the nearer part of the Avenue was built on the same sunrise alignment, and the pair of Heel Stones was enclosed by a narrow ditch, almost at once filled up again.

The Avenue provided the approach to Stonehenge. It is marked on the ground by two parallel ditches with banks on the inside. From the entrance to Stonehenge it passes the

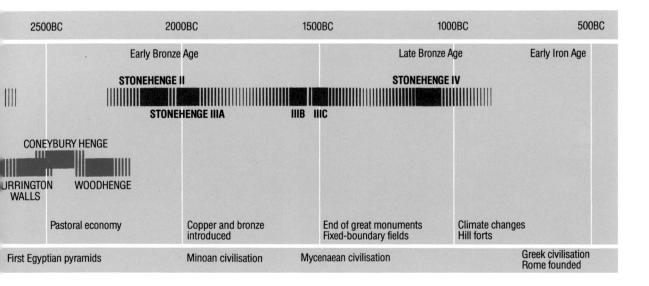

2500BC	2000BC	1500BC	1000BC	500BC
Early Bronze Age			Late Bronze Age	Early Iron Age

STONEHENGE II   STONEHENGE IV

STONEHENGE IIIA   IIIB   IIIC

CONEYBURY HENGE

DURRINGTON WALLS   WOODHENGE

Pastoral economy	Copper and bronze introduced	End of great monuments Fixed-boundary fields	Climate changes Hill forts	
First Egyptian pyramids	Minoan civilisation	Mycenaean civilisation		Greek civilisation Rome founded

Below *The third phase of Stonehenge about 2000BC saw the arrival of the sarsen stones. These were arranged in an outer circle with a continuous run of lintels. Inside the circle five trilithons were placed in a horseshoe arrangement, whose remains we can still see today. The axis of the monument pointed to the midsummer sunrise and was marked externally by a single Heel Stone inside a small circular ditch*

Below *The tallest sarsen, the remaining upright of the great central trilithon, weighs over 45 tonnes and is 22 feet high. Its fallen lintel lies in front. The mortice-and-tenon joints can be clearly seen in this photograph*

surviving Heel Stone and runs downhill for about 530m (1740ft) to the dry valley called Stonehenge Bottom.

This remodelling of Stonehenge was probably the work of local people. It looks as if the building of the double bluestone circle was still in progress when the decision was made, for reasons that we shall never know, to abandon it and to replace it by something much larger.

Arrival of the Sarsens

| 3000 BC | 2000 BC | 1000 BC |

This new structure, probably started about 2000 BC, was the lintelled circle and horseshoe of large sarsen stones, whose remains we can still see today. Its axis, like that of the unfinished double circle which it replaced, pointed to the midsummer sunrise and was marked externally by a single Heel Stone inside a small circular ditch, and internally by a pair of large stones set close together in the entrance of the earthwork, only one of which, the fallen Slaughter Stone, now survives.

This extraordinary building exhibits a number of refinements which cannot be found anywhere else amongst the prehistoric stone monuments of Europe, outside the Mediterranean area. First, all the stones have been squared and dressed to shape by pounding their surfaces with heavy stone hammers before they were erected. Second, the lintels are held in place on their uprights by mortice-and-tenon

Below *The side of this sarsen has been dressed by hammering shallow grooves to remove the rough surface of the natural stone*

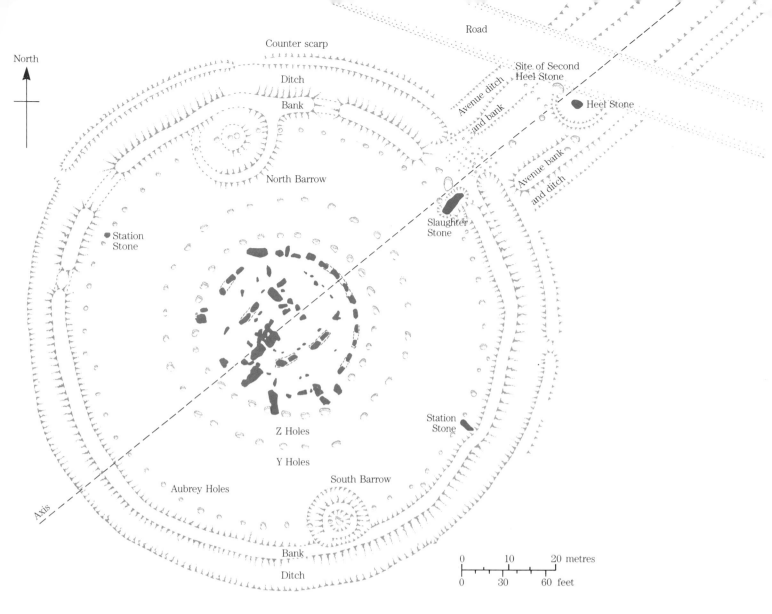

North

Road

Counter scarp

Ditch

Bank

Site of Second
Heel Stone

Heel Stone

Avenue ditch
and bank

North Barrow

Avenue bank
and ditch

Slaughter
Stone

Station
Stone

Station
Stone

Z Holes

Y Holes

South Barrow

Aubrey Holes

Axis

Bank

Ditch

0		10		20 metres
0		30		60 feet

joints, worked in the solid stone, and the lintels of the outer circle are locked end-to-end by vertical tongue-and-groove joints as well. Thirdly, the lintels themselves are not straight-sided blocks, but have their sides shaped to the curves on which they lie. Furthermore, the sides of the trilithon lintels are not vertical but are inclined towards the ground. These are all refinements of design which are peculiar to Stonehenge alone.

The jointing of the stones is probably imitated from woodworking methods, and we know that at much the same date huge timber structures were being erected close by at Woodhenge (p 33) and Durrington Walls (p 32). The upward taper of the sarsen pillars may likewise imitate the natural tapering form of tree-trunks; but it could possibly represent a deliberate though crude attempt to increase the apparent height of the stones by an optical illusion. Similarly the tilting of the sides of the

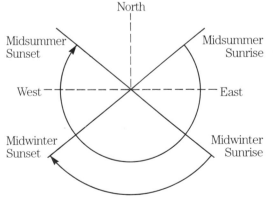

North

Midsummer
Sunset

Midsummer
Sunrise

West

East

Midwinter
Sunset

Midwinter
Sunrise

trilithon lintels does have the effect, and perhaps intentionally, of making them look as if they are vertical to an observer inside the horseshoe.

Given the size and weight of the stones, and

Above *General plan of Stonehenge showing outlying features, entrance and rings of excavated holes*

Left *The seasonal variation in the rising and setting of the sun in southern Britain*

11

Below *The next stage of Stonehenge involved the selection of about twenty bluestones, which were shaped and erected in an oval setting inside the sarsen horseshoe. At least two miniature copies in bluestone were made of the great sarsen trilithons. Their separated components still survive. Sometime later, around 1550BC, two rings of holes were dug (the Y and Z holes in the plan) to form once again a double circle of bluestones but the project was abandoned*

the primitive means available for moving, shaping and erecting them, this sarsen building of the Early Bronze Age represents one of the most remarkable and astonishing of all the achievements of prehistoric man in Europe.

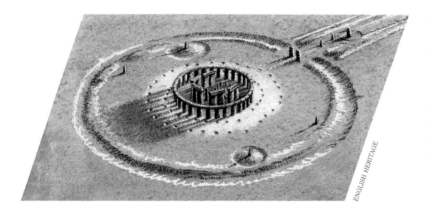

3000 BC   2000 BC   1000 BC

After the sarsen stones had been set up, rather more than twenty of the bluestones dismantled at the end of period II were selected, dressed to shape and erected in an oval setting on the line of the later bluestone horseshoe. Only a few of the stone-holes for this setting have so far been found in excavations, so that its exact plan is still uncertain. It does seem to have included, however, at least two miniature copies in bluestone of the great sarsen trilithons and the tongued-and-grooved pair, the separate components of which still survive, though re-used in a different way at a later date. One of the two bluestone lintels, now in the present bluestone circle, has marks of wear on its under side which show that it must have rested on its supporting pillar for a long time, perhaps for several centuries.

We do not know the date of this oval setting of dressed bluestones. It could have been part of the same design as the sarsen stones, and completed as soon as they had been set up. Equally, it could have been a fresh addition at a later date. In either case, however, it seems to have been the intention of the builders to make use in the end of the remaining 60 bluestones

Below *The final stage of Stonehenge took place soon after 1550BC when the bluestones were rearranged in the horseshoe and circle that we see the remains of today. About 80 bluestones were used, but very few survive. The largest bluestone, the Altar Stone probably stood as a tall pillar on the axial line of the monument*

left over from period II, which had not so far been dressed to shape. It is almost certainly to hold these that two rings of holes were dug about 1550 BC, to form once again a double circle. These are shown as the Y and Z holes on the plan, but are not visible.

For some unknown reason, however, this project too was abandoned, unfinished. The last few holes to be dug, on the east side, were irregular and incomplete, and no stones were ever set up in any of them. The design was abandoned, and the oval setting of bluestones in the centre was demolished.

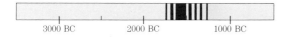

The final reconstruction of Stonehenge probably followed almost at once. The uprights of the former oval structure were reset in the horseshoe of bluestones that we can see the remains of today, and probably reshaped to their present alternating forms of pillar and obelisk. The remaining unshaped bluestones were erected in the present bluestone circle, together with the two bluestone lintels, re-used as pillars with the mortice-holes facing outwards so that they could not be seen from inside. Both have since fallen over in different directions, so that the mortices on one of them now lie underground. The original number of stones in the bluestone circle was probably about 60, set quite close together, but most of them have since been broken up or removed, or survive only as battered stumps below ground level.

The largest bluestone of all, the Altar Stone, probably stood as a tall pillar on the axial line inside the central and highest sarsen trilithon, and has since fallen down. There is no reason to suppose that its present position, or its name, is more than accidental.

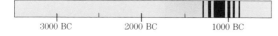

About 1100 BC the Avenue was extended from Stonehenge Bottom to pass over the hill to the east, and from there south-eastwards to the River Avon. This must mean that Stonehenge was still in use at that date, and presumably for some time afterwards, but we do not know for how long.

Beyond the dry valley the Avenue has long since been destroyed by ploughing. Its course was rediscovered by air-photography only about fifty years ago. Its total length is about 2,780m (3,040 yards).

North

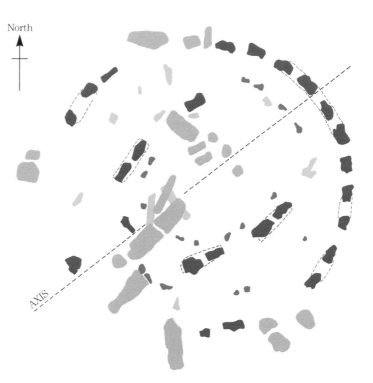

Stonehenge as it is today. Sarsen stones are shown in brown (upright) and beige (fallen). Bluestones in blue (upright) and pale blue (fallen). Lintels are outlined in a dotted line

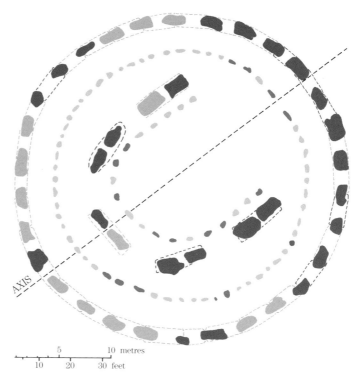

Stonehenge as it was. The stones are shown in their original positions. Sarsens are shown in brown (standing today) and beige (fallen or missing). Bluestones in blue (standing today) and pale blue (fallen or missing), Lintels are outlined in a dotted line

13

Carvings on the stones

Four of the sarsen uprights have prehistoric carvings on their sides. The earliest of these, high up on the inside face of the fourth trilithon of the horseshoe, is a shallow oblong shape similar to carvings found in Neolithic stone burial-chambers in Brittany, which are sometimes thought to represent in a simplified and symbolic way the figure of a mother-goddess. This carving is out of reach of the ground and was therefore made, probably, before the stone was set up.

Above *The shallow angular carving on the fourth trilithon resembles the mother-goddess symbols found in Neolithic burial chambers in Brittany*

The carvings on the other three stones are all nearer the ground, and made after the stones had been erected. Most of them are full-size representations of bronze axe-heads of the Early Bronze Age, of a kind commonly made in Britain and Ireland between 1800 BC and 1500 BC; but there is one carving also of a bronze dagger, the details of which are unlike those of contemproary British weapons. It could represent a foreign dagger, of the kind found in the Shaft Graves of Mycenae in Greece, the royal tombs of the legendary home of Agamemnon, dated around 1500 BC. At least one of the Early Bronze Age barrows near Stonehenge provides evidence of a similar link at the same date; but this identification of the carving at Stonehenge must remain a matter of opinion.

We shall never know for certain the reason for these carvings, but we can guess that these bronze weapons had some special significance as symbols, just as on many recent war-memorials a bronze sword stands both for the fallen soldier and for the Christian cross. All of them are now much weathered by time; but it is clear that they were shaped by abrasion with small stone hammers, much as the surfaces of the sarsen stones had themselves earlier been dressed smooth. Sarsen stone is far too hard to be cut with bronze chisels.

Below *Carvings on the second trilithon. The left-hand carving may represent a Mycenaean dagger, the right-hand a bronze axe-head*

How Stonehenge was built

Stonehenge is one of the most remarkable achievements of prehistoric engineering in Europe. For building it the only motive power was human muscles, aided by the simplest devices such as ropes, levers and rollers.

The ditch, the Aubrey Holes, and all the other holes for stones and posts were dug with pick-axes made from the antlers of red deer. The chalk rubble loosened with picks was scraped together with the shoulderblades of cattle and loaded into baskets so that it could be dumped where required. Wooden shovels may have been used as well, but no trace of them survives. Modern experiments have shown that these tools are more effective than they look. To dig the Stonehenge ditch and build the bank with them would have taken only twice the time required to do it today with steel picks, shovels and buckets.

The bluestones at Stonehenge certainly come from the Preseli Mountains in south-west Wales and from the shores of Milford Haven. Whether they were brought directly to Stonehenge, or to some intermediate point in the first instance, their transport over so long a distance is an astonishing feat. The map shows the most likely route. From the Preseli Mountains, where boulders of bluestone of all shapes and sizes lie on the surface, they would be dragged on sledges and rollers to the headwaters of Milford Haven. There they would be loaded on to rafts, and carried by water along the south coast of Wales and up the Rivers Avon

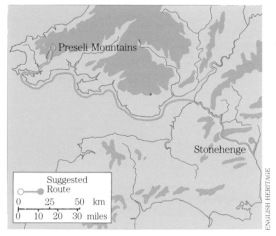

Left *The likely route of the bluestones from Preseli using water transport*

Suggested Route
0   25   50   km
0   10   20   30   miles

and Frome to near the modern town of Frome in Somerset. On the rivers, boats were probably used instead of rafts, which would have run aground in shallow water. From there they would be hauled overland again for about 10km (6 miles) to near Warminster in Wiltshire. Not far away there is a long barrow called Bowls Barrow in which a large block of bluestone has been found, built in to a central core of boulders. This long barrow was almost certainly constructed before 2900 BC, so that at least some bluestones must have arrived in the neighbourhood by that date. From here to Stonehenge the route is again mainly by water, down the River Wylye to Salisbury and up the Salisbury Avon to West Amesbury. The total distance is about 385km (240 miles).

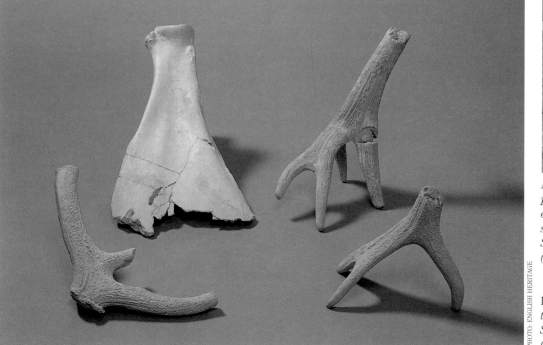

Above *Tip of antler pick found embedded in side of stone-hole at Stonehenge (Salisbury Museum)*

Left *Digging tools of the type used at Stonehenge (Salisbury Museum)*

15

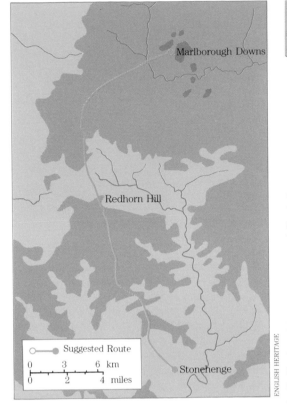

ENGLISH HERITAGE

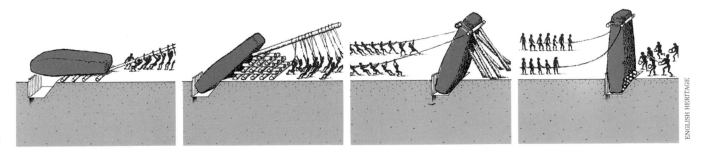

ENGLISH HERITAGE

Above *The stone lintels of the sarsen circle were linked horizontally by tongue-and-groove joints and secured vertically to the uprights by mortice-and-tenon joints*

The sarsen stones were almost certainly brought from the Marlborough Downs near Avebury in north Wiltshire, about 30km (20 miles) north of Stonehenge, where large blocks of the stone lie thickly on the surface. For these heavier stones water transport would be impossible, and they must have been dragged overland all the way on massive sledges and rollers, hauled with ropes of leather or cow-hair. The map shows the most probable route. Over most of its the slopes up and down are fairly easy; but at Redhorn Hill on the southern edge of the Vale of Pewsey the gradient is steep. To pull the heaviest stone, weighing about 50 tonnes, up this hill would have needed about 500 men, with an extra hundred at least to lay the rollers in front of the sledge and keep it from wandering sideways. Modern work studies suggest that even if all 600 men had been continuously employed over the complete route, the task would have taken more than a year to complete.

At Stonehenge itself the uprights and lintels were dressed to shape by pounding their surfaces with heavy sarsen hammers about the size of a football, many of which were later used as packing-stones round the bases of the uprights. The hollow mortices in the lintels were made in the same way. The tops of the stones must have been dressed level, leaving the tenons projecting, only after the uprights had been raised and given time to settle in the chalk. This was slow work, because sarsen stone is exceptionally hard and will turn the cutting edge even of modern steel tools.

The method probably used to erect the stones is shown below. A foundation pit was dug in the chalk, with one side vertical and the opposite one of the form of a sloping ramp. A row of wooden stakes was driven in against the vertical side to stop the chalk being crushed down by the toe of the stone as it was raised. The stone, base foremost, was then moved on rollers towards the ramp, until its toe was over the hole and its centre of gravity was just behind the leading roller. The outer end was then levered

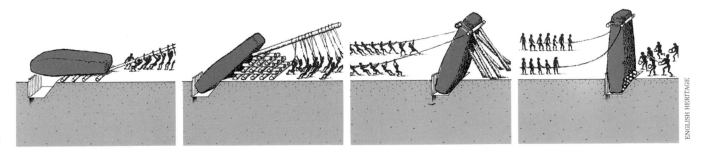

ENGLISH HERITAGE

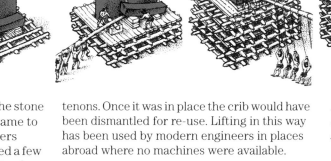

up, dipping the base into the hole, until the stone over-balanced at the last moment and came to rest in a leaning position. Next, with levers supported by timber packing, it was raised a few inches at a time and held in place by struts when the packing had to be rebuilt closer to the stone. Finally it would be pulled upright by gangs of men hauling on ropes. To raise a stone of the outer circle of sarsens would need about 200 men.

To help in adjusting the stones to a vertical position, their bases were dressed to a blunt point on which the mass could more easily pivot. When the final adjustment had been made, the hole round the base was rapidly packed with stones, including discarded hammers, and with chalk rammed hard.

The method probably used to raise the lintels is shown above. First the lintel is positioned on the ground, close and parallel to the base of the uprights, and each end alternately is lifted with levers and supported on temporary packing of squared timber. Then a 'crib' of criss-crossed timbers is built around the lintel and uprights, and decked over with stout planks just beneath the underside of the lintel. Now the weight of the stone is transferred with levers from the old packing resting on the ground to new packing resting on the deck. Thereafter the whole process is repeated in stages, the lintel being raised about 60cm (2ft) at each stage. Finally when the uppermost deck was level with the tops of the uprights the lintel is levered sideways to fit over the projecting

tenons. Once it was in place the crib would have been dismantled for re-use. Lifting in this way has been used by modern engineers in places abroad where no machines were available.

Destruction of Stonehenge

The final rebuilding of Stonehenge took place about 1550 BC. Its subsequent history is one of ruin, damage and destruction. In spite of their great size, many of the sarsen stones have disappeared. We know, however, that their builders were trying to achieve the maximum overall height with the material available, so that many of them stood in dangerously shallow holes and probably fell over at an early date. Moreover, there is no natural building stone within 21km (13 miles) of Stonehenge, so that in the Middle Ages, if not before, the fallen stones and the lintels (which could be levered or pulled off their uprights fairly easily) must have provided a convenient quarry for local builders.

The disappearance of so many of the bluestones, or their survival only as stumps below ground level, is easy to understand, because they are smaller and more brittle than the sarsens, and thus easier to pull down or break up with hammers. Much of the destruction is certainly due to earlier visitors, who delighted in knocking off fragments as

Above Raising a lintel to the top of two sarsens

Below Sarsen hammer-stones found at Stonehenge. They vary from a tennis-ball to a football in size. They were used for shaping the stones and later as packing around the base of the uprights (Salisbury Museum)

PHOTOS ENGLISH HERITAGE

keepsakes. Indeed at one time a hammer could be readily hired at the blacksmith's forge in Amesbury for this very purpose. It is known too that up to about a century ago the local farmers used to break up the bluestones and the fallen sarsens for road metal, to repair farm tracks and gateways.

Until 1918, when it was given to the nation, Stonehenge was in private hands. Since that date about half of the site has been excavated at various times, and a number of the leaning and fallen stones have been straightened and re-erected. In recent years the number of visitors has become so large (half a million in a year) that the surface of the monument, right out to the surrounding bank and ditch, has been dangerously eroded, and many of the fallen stones, and the stumps which protrude above the surface, are being ground away by the feet of those who step or climb on them. It has thus become necessary to prevent further erosion by restricting public access to the interior of the site. Only in this way can this unique structure be preserved for the future.

The Druids

Three hundred years ago the antiquary John Aubrey first suggested that stone circles were Druidical temples, and ever since it has been popularly believed that Stonehenge was built and used by the Druids. This belief is certainly false. Everything that we know about the Druids was recorded by classical writers like Julius Caesar, who tell us that they were a Celtic priesthood who flourished in Britain at the time of the Roman conquest, and perhaps for a few centuries before. By then the stones of Stonehenge had been standing for two thousand years, and were probably already in ruins. Moreover, these accounts make it clear that the Druids built no temples of their own, but held their ceremonies in clearings in the forest.

It may be, however, that the Druids inherited the knowledge and observations of natural events, astronomy included, of the builders of Stonehenge, handed down over the centuries by word of mouth. We are told that the Druids' lore was enshrined in a series of interminable verses, which a novice might take up to twenty years to learn by heart. Since there is no evidence from prehistoric Britain for any method of writing, or

Right *John Constable's painting of 1835, which was exhibited at the Royal Academy in 1836. Despite its appearance, the painting was not painted on the spot, but developed in his studio from a pencil sketch made in 1820*

18

of writing down numbers, this is one way in which such knowledge could have been stored and then passed on from one generation to the next. We know, for instance, that in the Pacific today accurate sailing-directions for very long voyages have been handed down by word of mouth alone over a period of many centuries.

Astronomy at Stonehenge

Ever since the early eighteenth century it has been recognised that the axis of the sarsen stones points roughly to where an observer at the centre of Stonehenge would see the sun rise on the longest day of the year, in its most northerly position on the horizon. The entrance was also reorientated slightly during the lifetime of Stonehenge to compensate for astronomical variation in the midsummer sunrise over many centuries.

More recently it has been suggested that the lines joining the four Station Stones could also have marked the most northerly and southerly positions on the horizon of the risings and settings of the sun and the moon, and that the latitude of Stonehenge was chosen so that pairs of these directions would be at right angles. In addition, the theory has been advanced that the ring of Aubrey Holes could have been used as a simplified model of the motions of the sun and moon, so as to predict eclipses; and it has also been claimed that Stonehenge served as an observatory for very precise observations of the extreme risings and settings of the moon.

Studies of other stone circles in Britain as well as Stonehenge itself have indicated that most, if not all, of these alignments are fortuitous and were not intended by the Neolithic and Bronze Age peoples who raised the stones. Alignments were symbolic rather than scientific in intent, although in many cases they were linked in general terms with the directions of the risings and settings of the sun. The use of Stonehenge as an astronomical observatory in prehistoric times will remain a matter for conjecture, but the claim is not supported by the archaeological record.

ADAM WOOLFTT (SUSAN GRIGGS)

Here oft, when Evening sheds her twilight ray,
And gilds with fainter beam departing day,
With breathless gaze, and cheek with terror pale,
The lingering shepherd startles at the tale,
How, at deep midnight, by the moon's chill glance,
Unearthly forms prolong the viewless dance;
While on each whisp'ring breeze that murmurs by,
His busied fancy hears the hollow sigh.

from 'Stonehenge' by Thomas Stokes Salmon, 1823

The Prehistoric Peoples

For many thousands of years, up to about 4000 BC, the people living in southern Britain consisted of scattered bands of roving hunters living on game, fish from the rivers and wild plants. They grew no crops and had no domesticated animals. For tools and weapons they used flint, bone and deer antler, and for shelter they built huts or wind-breaks of brushwood at their temporary camp-sites, and perhaps used skin tents as well.

The landscape at this time was very different from that of today, with broad tracts of dense woodland and hardly any open grassland. It would have supported only a tiny population of hunters.

By 4000 BC, however, Britain was inhabited by groups who practised an early form of farming. They cultivated primitive cereals and kept domesticated animals such as sheep, goats, pigs, cattle and dogs. They established their farms throughout Britain and Ireland, including the chalk lands of Wessex, where the remains of their settlements, burial mounds and ritual enclosures have been found.

They lived by herding their animals, growing grain and by exchange of commodities, mainly raw materials. Their farms were located in small irregular plots, which were probably sown with a crop year after year until the fertility of the soil was exhausted. Then the families concerned would clear new plots from the forest and scrub.

No houses of the period survive for certain in Wiltshire, but we know from discoveries elsewhere that they were long and rectangular, and large enough for an extended family and their animals.

Their tools and hunting weapons were mostly of flint, which was obtained from surface outcrops and river beds, or by digging shafts into the chalk. Axes were specially important for the clearing of woodland and the shaping of timber for houses. As well as the good local flint, there is evidence that the axes were also made from stone imported as far distant as Cumbria, North Wales and Cornwall.

Their clothes were of leather (like the suede used today), although evidence of weaving suggests that cloth was worn as well. Hide was probably used for some of their domestic utensils, though excavations elsewhere suggest most would have been of wood. Small implements were of antler and bone. Their baggy round-bottomed pots look like imitations in clay of the leather vessels. They buried their important dead in specially constructed narrow mounds called long barrows.

Pottery and tools of the period before Stonehenge. The pottery (top) *imitates earlier leather vessels (Devizes Museum). Axes were usually made of polished flint* (bottom), *but could also be of imported volcanic stone* (centre) *from western Britain (Salisbury Museum). Tools for working leather and textiles* (lower right) *were carved from antler or bone (Avebury Museum)*

After the first settlement, these early Neolithic farmers probably grew in numbers fairly quickly, because unlike the native hunters, who had to live from hand to mouth, they could build up a store of surplus food in the form of grain and of meat on the hoof. In time this increased population had a marked effect on the landscape, through the replacement of forest by open grassland and by thickets of scrub. This was brought about partly by the deliberate clearance of woodland, but mainly by prolonged grazing in the forests. Animals nibbled the bark of young saplings and pigs grubbed up their roots, so that when old trees died they were not replaced by new ones. By late Neolithic times, from about 3000 BC, much of the original forest had disappeared and the landscape was beginning to appear more open. By this time too the population had grown so much that labour could be spared for communal works.

Above *Stone mace-head, a fragment of pottery and two bone tools, found in four of the Aubrey Holes at Stonehenge (Salisbury Museum)*

Right *Artist's impression of the Stonehenge landscape about 3000BC. The newly built chalk bank of the first Stonehenge can be seen beyond the trees*

23

Soon after 2500 BC a new pastoral economy developed in eastern and southern Britain. Groups of immigrants may have crossed the North Sea from the Rhineland, but archaeologically there is no detectable evidence of immigration. The new culture is known as 'Beaker' from the common occurrence of pottery drinking-vessels found in graves. The changes may have been merely the adaptation by local peoples of imported ideas.

Around this time the working and use of the first metals were introduced. The main sources of these metals lay in Ireland. It was probably the demand for these metals that opened up the trade routes to Wessex and other parts of Britain, and thus laid the foundations of the British bronze industry which was to last for nearly another two thousand years.

A new custom widely adopted by the population was the burial of the dead singly under a round mound or barrow, with a beaker or drinking-vessel and sometimes with a copper knife or a bow and arrows tipped with flint. From this time onwards, up to about 1500 BC, burial under a round barrow became the almost universal practice for people of importance, and one nowhere better seen than in the landscape around Stonehenge.

Left *Stone axe-hammers, possibly intended for ceremonial use rather than as real tools (Salisbury Museum)*

PHOTO: ENGLISH HERITAGE

Right *Artist's impression of the Stonehenge landscape about 2000BC. The land has been largely cleared of trees. Chalk burial mounds of local chieftains can be seen on the skyline*

Left *Skeleton of a man buried about 2000BC, when the bluestones were brought to Stonehenge. He holds a pottery drinking vessel and was buried with his bronze dagger (Salisbury Museum)*

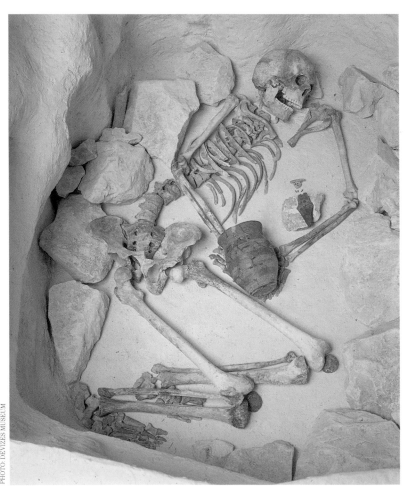

PHOTO: DEVIZES MUSEUM

PHOTOS: ENGLISH HERITAGE

Above *Bronze dagger, with replica haft, similar to burial on left (Devizes Museum)*

Above *Barbed flint arrowheads, imitating metal originals (Salisbury Museum)*

ENGLISH HERITAGE

PHOTOS: ENGLISH HERITAGE

Above *Copper and bronze daggers of the early Bronze Age (Devizes Museum)*

Above *Pottery drinking vessels of the late Neolithic and early Bronze Age periods (Devizes Museum)*

25

Above *Artist's impression of the erection of the sarsen temple about 2000BC. In the left background a stone arrives on a sledge pulled on rollers; other stones are being hauled upright or capped with lintels. In the foreground, the surveyors receive instructions. Many of the items shown can be seen in the Salisbury and Devizes Museums*

Left *Pottery funerary vessels of the early Bronze Age, of the sort found in burial mounds surrounding Stonehenge (Devizes Museum)*

Above Grave goods of gold, bronze and bone, from an early Bronze Age burial mound (Devizes Museum)

Below Gold-plated ornaments of amber and shale, from a burial mound near Stonehenge (Devizes Museum)

By about 2000 BC the growing use of bronze for tools and weapons, made by alloying copper from the west of Britain and from Ireland with tin from Cornwall, and the continued increase in grazing land as the old forests shrank, led to the rise in Wessex of a numerous population apparently dominated by a number of ruling families. Their wealth was probably due mainly to their success as farmers. But it owed something too, perhaps, to their controlling position on one of the trade-routes between Ireland and the nearer parts of Europe, to which bronze tools and gold ornaments were now being exported. The barrow-burials of the leading families, which cluster thickly in cemeteries around Stonehenge, contain objects which show connections with Brittany, Holland and central Europe. It is clear that at this time Britain was more truly a part of Europe than at any later prehistoric period. It was these rich families of Salisbury Plain with their interests in the metal trade who commanded the resources and the authority to raise the great stones of Stonehenge. About 1500 BC this rich community seems to have suffered a rapid decline. Signs of wealth and aristocracy begin to disappear. The reasons for this change are unknown, though perhaps the adoption of a new pattern of farming may have had something to do with it. The growing of grain, mainly barley, on fields with permanent boundaries, and the use of manure to restore the fertility of soils cultivated on some kind of rotation of crops, probably reduced the amount of spare time that could have been used for communal works. It is clear that after about 1500 BC the Stonehenge region as a whole began to lose the special importance as a centre of religion and of political power which it had possessed for the last two thousand years.

After this date, only a very few round barrows were added to the long-established cemeteries which lie all around Stonehenge, and no new major monuments were built. None the less, the Stonehenge Avenue was extended about 1100 BC, which must mean that Stonehenge itself was still known and respected both then and for some unknown period afterwards, and that it retained its special importance. Few other prehistoric monuments in Britain have so long a history of almost continuous use as Stonehenge, despite the many changes that must have taken place in the economy and social structure, and perhaps even in the religious beliefs, of the people who used it.

27

The Stonehenge Area

To give the reader as complete a picture as possible, all the major prehistoric monuments of the Neolithic period and the beginning of the Bronze Age in the Stonehenge area are described and illustrated in this guide. Some of them, however, including many of the long and round barrows, lie on private land or in a military area and cannot be visited by the public.

The landscape for a few miles around Stonehenge contains more prehistoric remains than any other area of the same size in Britain. Their positions are shown in the map, and the table on pages 8 and 9 gives their dates.

These dates are based mainly on the radiocarbon process, which can measure the age of specimens of animal or vegetable material found in excavations, usually in the form of wood charcoal, animal bones or deer antlers. Dates obtained in this way are rough ones only, with a margin of uncertainty of several centuries either way. They do allow us, however, to arrange the various monuments more or less in the order in which they were built and used.

The monuments themselves are of several different kinds, with different purposes. The most numerous – the long barrows of the Neolithic period and the round barrows of the Bronze Age – are burial places. The 'causewayed camp' at Robin Hood's Ball is probably a ceremonial enclosure for tribal meetings. The Cursus seems to be a ritual enclosure of another sort, perhaps for processions or races. The four 'henge monuments' – Stonehenge, Woodhenge, Coneybury and Durrington Walls – are generally thought to be prehistoric temples, though we shall never know how they were used or what religious beliefs they represent. Few prehistoric houses or other domestic sites have so far been found in the area, but there is a group of flint mines close to Durrington Walls and flint quarries to the south of Stonehenge.

Most of these monuments have been partially excavated at various times over the last two centuries. As a result of these explorations, and of similar ones elsewhere, it is possible to describe in outline the way of life of the people who built and used them (see 'Prehistoric Peoples' on pages 21-27). Because the monuments belong to the prehistoric period, however, long before any written records were made, there are many questions about them that we shall never be able to answer. The evidence consists of fragmentary remains of structures, long ruined and decayed, and mostly underground, and of objects of stone, metal,

Opposite
*Stonehenge as seen
from the Slaughter
Stone (foreground)*

pottery and bone, many of them no more than scraps of former rubbish. Wood, leather, cloth and other organic materials have mostly vanished. The archaeologist can now study only a small and very incomplete part of what originally existed.

From this evidence it is often possible to say **how** things were made or built, and in some cases to tell **when** and **by whom**. It is hardly ever possible to answer the question **why**.

Robin Hood's Ball

This eroded earthwork lies on a slight rise in the chalk downland about 4.3km (2.7 miles) north-north-west of Stonehenge, in a military area closed to the public. Two irregular rings of bank and ditch enclose an oval space of about 1 hectare (2.5 acres), both ditches being broken by unexcavated causeways of solid chalk.

This is probably the earliest prehistoric site in the area, and the only local example of a Neolithic 'causewayed enclosure', of which about fifty have been found on the chalk and the valley gravels of southern and eastern England. They date from about 4000 to 3300 BC, and they probably served as meeting-places.

The ditches of some enclosures have yielded human remains – particularly skulls – suggesting that they played some part in an elaborate funerary ritual. It seems probable that the enclosures served a multiplicity of purposes, which today would be served by the town hall, the magistrates' court and even, possibly, by the church or chapel.

The limited excavations at Robin Hood's Ball have not shown whether there were buildings within the enclosure; but we can be fairly sure that this was the first 'community centre' in the area, long before anything was built at Stonehenge.

Long Barrows

Throughout the chalk of Wessex and Sussex, and further north in Lincolnshire and east Yorkshire, the early Neolithic farmers buried their important dead in long barrows, of which over 200 are known in these areas. Fifteen of them lie within a radius of about 5km (3 miles) of Stonehenge, a larger number than in any area of the same size elsewhere. This suggests that the neighbourhood was one of special importance or sanctity even before Stonehenge itself was built.

The long barrows of the area vary in length from 20m (65ft) to 80m (265ft), and all but one of them exceeds 30m (100ft). Their width varies even more, but is usually between one-sixth and one-third of the length, as originally built. Allowance must be made for the spreading of the mound sideways as the result of thousands of years of weathering and erosion. Originally the mounds of chalk, excavated from ditches with flat bottoms and almost vertical sides, parallel with the edges of the barrow, stood up to 3m (10ft) in height. In some cases the sides of the mound were parallel, and in others one end was broader and higher than the other.

Many of the long barrows in the area were partially excavated in the nineteenth century, but the records of these explorations do not allow us to reconstruct the ritual of burial. More recent excavations elsewhere, however, show that the bodies of the dead were kept above ground for some time, and in some cases were exposed on raised timber platforms where they would be out of reach of animals but would soon be picked clean by birds of prey. Only after some years, and perhaps when some one of special importance had died, were the bones collected and laid on the ground, sometimes inside a low mortuary building of timber. Then the long mound of chalk was piled over them, the bones lying towards one end which usually faced roughly towards the east.

The best-preserved long barrow in the area lies on private land just to the north-east of the roundabout at the Winterbourne Stoke crossroads, on the A303 about 2.4km (1.5 miles) from Stonehenge. It can be seen from the road to the east of the roundabout. Pedestrians should use the NT footpath rather than walk the length of the A303 from Stonehenge (see map opposite). This long barrow is typical of its kind in Wessex. It contains over 1500 cubic metres (53000 cubic feet) of chalk. With the primitive tools available it would have taken a dozen people about four months to build, if they worked for eight hours every day.

None of the long barrows in the area has been dated directly, but examples elsewhere in Wessex suggest that they were built between about 4000 BC and 3000 BC. A long barrow may have been the tomb of all the members of a single family (apart from children who died very young), but was more likely used only for the burial of selected people if special importance, belonging to a group of neighbouring or related families.

Flint Mines

The main material used for tools and hunting weapons by the Neolithic farmers was flint, which occurs at various levels in the chalk in the form of seams of large lumps or nodules or along river beds. Surface flint is often cracked by frost and is unsuitable for making large tools. Better quality raw material had to be mined by sinking shafts into the chalk.

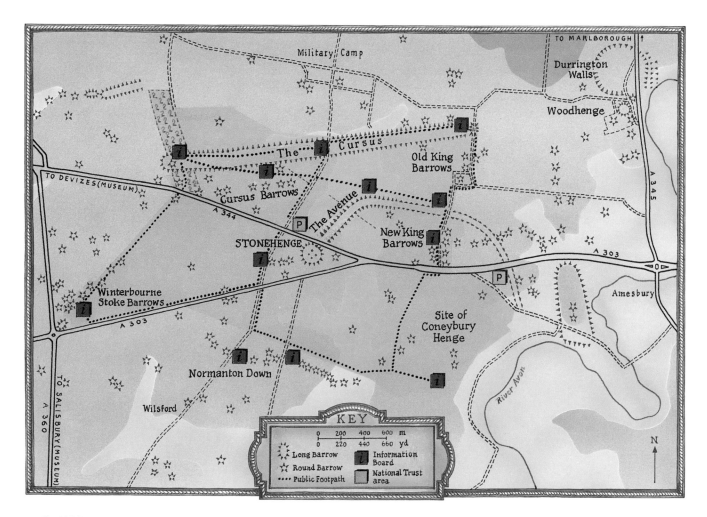

Map labels (clockwise):

TO MARLBOROUGH

Military Camp

Durrington Walls

Woodhenge

The Cursus

Old King Barrows

A 345

TO DEVIZES (MUSEUM)

Cursus Barrows

The Avenue

New King Barrows

A 344

STONEHENGE

A 303

Winterbourne Stoke Barrows

A 303

Site of Coneybury Henge

Amesbury

P

Normanton Down

River Avon

Wilsford

TO SALISBURY (MUSEUM)

A 360

N

KEY

0	200	400	600	m
0	220	440	660	yd

Long Barrow
Round Barrow
Public Footpath
Information Board
National Trust area

In 1952 a sewer-trench to the north-east of Durrington Walls (p 32) cut through part of a flint-mining area. Three broad shallow pits had evidently been dug to exploit a seam of flint very close to the surface, which was probably of poor quality. Two other shafts had been dug to a depth of 2.2m (7.2ft), with low galleries extending from the bottom to follow a deeper seam. The full extent of this mining area is unknown, and the site is now covered by houses and gardens.

Flint for everyday tools seems to have been obtained from a flint seam that outcrops on the sides of dry valleys to south of Stonehenge. Excavations here revealed rejected flints and hammerstones, which indicate the flint quarry was much used.

The Cursus

This extraordinary earthwork lies about 800m (875 yards) to the north of Stonehenge. It consists of a narrow enclosure 2.8km (1.75 miles) long and 90m (100 yards) wide, marked out on either side by a small bank with a ditch outside, much of which has been flattened by ploughing. To the west, just beyond Fargo Plantation, it was closed by a rounded end where the ditch and bank were deeper and higher than elsewhere. To the east it was aligned on a long barrow of earlier date, which has been worn away by a modern track which passes over it. The Cursus can be visited by following the way-marked trail from the Stonehenge car-park.

Elsewhere in southern and eastern England a number of similar earthworks have been discovered. Some of these are also aligned on earlier long barrows, and some have been firmly dated to the Middle Neolithic period by excavation. Their purpose is unknown; but their unusual shape suggests that they were ceremonial or religious enclosures, intended perhaps for processions or for ritual races connected with the honouring of dead ancestors.

The name 'Cursus' was first given to this earthwork by the eighteenth-century antiquary William Stukeley, who thought that it was a race-course for the chariots of the Ancient Britons. We know now that it is of much earlier date. It may have been the religious centre of the

Above *Map showing the prehistoric barrows and monuments of the Stonehenge area. Most of these can be visited*

31

Stonehenge area before Stonehenge itself was built.

To the west of Fargo Plantation there are the remains of a much smaller Cursus, now almost invisible, which is rounded at the west end, open at the east end and divided in the centre by a transverse ditch. It is shorter than most of the other Cursus monuments. Excavations have shown it was built in two stages but have not thrown any light on its function. It lies on private land, not open to visitors.

Durrington Walls

The earthwork of Durrington Walls lies immediately north of Woodhenge (see map on page 31) spanning a dry valley. It has been much altered and damaged by ploughing in the past.

It consisted of a huge, roughly oval bank of chalk, about 30m (100ft) wide at the base and 3m (10ft) high, built from material dug out of a ditch on the inside. There were entrances on opposite sides, the lower one being close to the River Avon. The site was first occupied from

Below *Aerial photograph of the Cursus, with Stonehenge in the background. See key for details*

about 3200 BC and the earthwork was built around 2550 BC.

The strip of land beneath the embankment of the new road was excavated in 1966-68, and revealed the remains of two circular timber structures. The northern structure may have been a round thatched building about 14.5m (48ft) across, with a roof raised in the centre to admit light and air. It was built about 2450 BC, and may have replaced an earlier building.

The southern structure revealed the remains of two successive buildings of timber. The earlier one was about 23m (75ft) in diameter. It may have been roofed right across; but more probably it had a ring-shaped roof sloping inwards, enclosing an open space. The later building had six circles of posts, the outer one being 39m (128ft) in diameter. It was built about 2450 BC, and was probably roofed with an open space at the centre, like Woodhenge.

Large amounts of decorated pottery and animal bones were found during the excavations. They point to some special ceremonial activities taking place here.

Durrington Walls, like Stonehenge, gives us an idea of the amount of labour devoted by the Late Neolithic people to communal works. To build the earthwork would require nearly a million man-hours, or 100 men working six days a week for four years. The largest tree trunks would have been over 1m (3.3ft) in diameter and could have weighed nearly 11 tonnes.

Woodhenge

Woodhenge lies about 3km (2 miles) to the north-east of Stonehenge, just to the west of the A345. It was formerly supposed to be the site of a destroyed disc-barrow (p 35); but aerial photographs taken in 1925 showed rings of dark spots in a crop of wheat. This suggested that there were holes underground in which wooden posts had stood, a fact confirmed when the site was excavated soon afterwards. The positions of the wooden posts are now marked by concrete blocks.

The outer boundary consisted of a circular bank, now almost flattened by ploughing, with a broad flat-bottomed ditch inside it, originally about 2.5m (8ft) in depth, and an entrance-gap on the north-north-east side. This earthwork was built about 2300 BC.

On the flat area inside the ditch the excavators found six concentric oval rings of circular holes, which had held wooden posts of varying size.

Near the centre there was a grave (now marked by a small cairn of flints) containing the body of a three-year-old whose skull had been split before burial. This was perhaps a

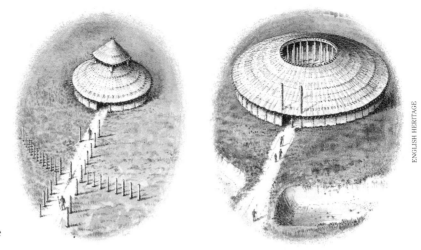

Above *Likely reconstructions of two buildings inside Durrington Walls. The left-hand drawing shows the northern structure. The right-hand illustration is of the larger southern structure: a building of this sort may have stood at the centre of the first Stonehenge*

dedicatory burial, and is one of the very few pieces of evidence for human sacrifice in Neolithic Britain.

Since only their ground-plan is known, it is difficult to reconstruct the rings of posts with any certainty. They may have stood in the open, carved and painted, and perhaps with their tops joined by lintels at different levels, like the stones of Stonehenge. On the other hand, they may be the uprights of a roofed building. As the largest posts are in the third ring, this would

Grooved ware vessel excavated at Durrington Walls (Salisbury Museum)

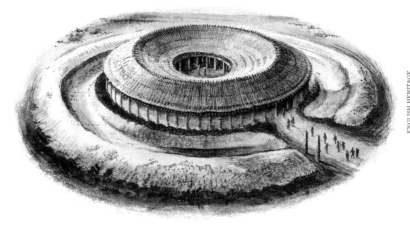

Above *Possible reconstruction illustration of Woodhenge. Inside the earthwork were rings of post-holes. How the posts were used is merely guess-work, but they make best sense as the framework of a circular building. The thickest and highest timbers could have supported the ridge of the roof, and the eaves would have rested on smaller posts, leaving an open light well in the centre*

Above *Symbolic chalk axes excavated at Woodhenge (Devizes Museum)*

probably have looked like a huge thatched barn bent round on itself, leaving an open space in the centre.

Whatever its original form, this timber structure was probably a temple, a tribal meeting-place or a combination of both. The discovery of symbolic axe-heads carved out of soft chalk, buried in post-holes of the two outer rings at Woodhenge, hints at its use for a special or religious purpose in which axes had a special meaning. The bronze axe-heads carved at Stonehenge (p 14) show the long-continued use of the axe as a symbol.

Coneybury Henge

Coneybury Hill lies 1.3km (0.8 mile) south-east of Stonehenge in a heavily cultivated area. Nothing can be seen on the ground and access is limited to the way-marked path shown on the map.

The true nature of this 'henge monument' was first disclosed from analysis of aerial photography. Excavations in 1980 have revealed evidence of a circular ditch which enclosed a complex of post-holes and pits, some of which contained late Neolithic pottery. Scatters of flint tools have been found in the surrounding fields. Excavations in 1983 just north of Coneybury found proof of domestic activity.

Coneybury Henge appears to have been used for only a very short time before it was abandoned. Its short occupation period relates to the phase when Stonehenge itself was abandoned after Period I (see page 8) and other sites, such as Woodhenge and Durrington Walls, were built.

Round Barrows

All round Stonehenge the landscape is dotted with round barrows, the burial-mounds of the people of the Early Bronze Age. Many have now been flattened by ploughing, so that originally they were even more numerous than they appear today. Even now we can see more barrows within 3km (2 miles) of Stonehenge than in any other area of the same size in Britain.

Many of them are grouped in cemeteries strung out in a line along a ridge. One of the largest of these can be seen from Stonehenge on the crest of Normanton Down, 800m (0.5 miles) to the south. For a closer look, a way-marked track leads from the Stonehenge car-park.

Another group, the Cursus Barrows, stands on the rising ground to the north-west, and a third, the King Barrows, is concealed in two beech woods on the skyline to the east. Way-marked paths similarly lead to these barrow-groups.

A well-preserved barrow-cemetery runs north-eastwards from the roundabout on the A303 at Winterbourne Stoke cross-roads 2.4km (1.5 miles) from Stonehenge. The barrows are best seen from the way-marked path shown on the map, as walking along the main road can be dangerous. The barrow-cemetery contains examples of all the main kinds of round barrow to be found in the Stonehenge area. Those furthest from the cross-roads are simple bowl-shaped mounds, with or without a surrounding ditch, known as **bowl-barrows**. Nearer the cross-roads, close to the edge of the wood, there are two **bell-barrows**, with the edge of the large mound separated from the surrounding ditch by a flat space.

Overlapping the ditch of the bell barrow nearer the cross-roads is a **pond-barrow**, a rare type in which a central circular hollow is surrounded by a ring-shaped bank. Only about forty of these are known altogether, all of them in Wessex. Some contain burials; others enclose a flint pavement on which ceremonies to honour the near-by dead may have been conducted.

North of the bell-barrows, and outside the main line, there are two **disc barrows**, with small mounds surrounded at a distance by a ditch with an outer bank. Near them to the north-east is a ditched bowl barrow and a second pond barrow, larger than the first.

The main line of barrows is one the axis of the earlier Neolithic long barrow close to the roundabout. This suggests the possible continuous use of the same cemetery, over a period of 1500 years or more, for the burial of the most important members of some ruling family. The other barrow cemeteries in the area are probably of the same special kind, and are thought not to represent the burials of the population at large. It is clear that where barrows are set in a long straight line, the disc barrows always lie to one side, indicating they are of a slightly later date.

Most of these barrows around Stonehenge were partially excavated at the beginning of the nineteenth century, and the objects deposited in the graves can be seen in the Devizes and Salisbury Museums. Men were often buried with weapons such as bronze daggers, bronze tomahawks and stone battle-axes, which can be regarded as symbols of rank and authority, like the sword worn by senior officers of the armed forces on special ceremonial occasions today. Women's graves contain bead necklaces and other ornaments. At the beginning of the Bronze Age the bodies of the dead were usually buried in a crouched position in a grave cut in the chalk. Later the cremation of the body on a funeral pyre became increasingly common, and eventually universal, the burned ashes being

deposited in a small pit or in a pottery urn before the barrow was heaped up over them. Sometimes later burials were inserted into the mounds of existing barrows. There are also flat graves between barrows.

In spite of their exceptional number, the barrows round Stonehenge can only be in burial-places of the leading members of the leading families in each generation – the ruling class who had the wealth and the power to command the transport and erection of the bluestones and the sarsens at Stonehenge. They are not the burials of the common people who did the work, whose only memorial is Stonehenge itself.

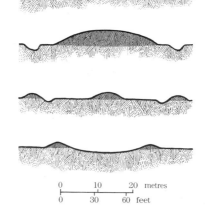

0   10   20 metres
0   30   60 feet

Above *Aerial photograph of barrows at Winterbourne Stoke cross-roads. Details are shown in the key*

Left *Four types of round barrow. From top: bowl, bell, disc and pond*

35

Local Museums

Objects illustrated in this guidebook are credited in the caption with the name of the museum where they can be seen.

Of the county museums, the following are recommended, but visitors are advised to check hours of admission in advance before making a long journey.

Salisbury and South Wiltshire Museum

The King's House, 65 The Close, Salisbury SP1 2EN

Open: Mon-Sat (and Sun afternoons in July and August)
Telephone: 0722 332151
Items from the excavations in the Stonehenge Gallery and a special exhibit on Early Man in Wiltshire.

Devizes Museum

The Wiltshire Archaeological and Natural History Society
41 Long Street, Devizes SN10 1NS

Open: Tues-Sat
Telephone: 0380 77369
Artefacts from the barrows and other prehistoric collections. Henge Monument Room.

Alexander Keiller Museum Avebury

Avebury, Marlborough SN8 1RF

Open: Mon-Sun
Telephone: 067 23250
Flints and pottery from excavations at Avebury, Windmill Hill, Silbury Hill and West Kennet.

Below *William Cunnington, the antiquarian, driving home from an expedition to Stonehenge in about 1802. His daughter is seen clutching the day's find, a large urn from a barrow. Many of the objects found are now in museums*